THROUGH THE MONEY MAZE

Brian Dick

informe Limited

© Anforme Ltd., 1984.

ISBN 0 907529 13 5

Anforme Ltd.,
Pennine House, 4 Osborne Tce.,
Newcastle upon Tyne NE2 1NE

Cover design and print by
Unit Offset Ltd.,
Brunswick Industrial Estate,
Newcastle upon Tyne NE13 7BA

CONTENTS

Chapter		Page
1	The Theory of Money Demand	1
2	The Money Transmissions Mechanism	7
3	But What is Money?	10
4	The Adoption of the Monetarist Philosophy in the UK	14
5	The Operation of Monetarism in the UK	19
6	Money Markets and the Structure of Interest Rates	26
7	Monetary Targeting in the UK	33
Appendix 1	Provisions of Competition and Credit Control	39
Appendix 2	The Expectations-Augmented Phillips Curve and the Natural Rate of Unemployment	41
Notes		47
References		49

INTRODUCTION

Monetary theory and the institutional structure through which monetary policy is implemented seems to be one of those areas of the economics syllabus with which students have greatest difficulty. Questions on this area in the G.C.E. examination papers in particular are not popular with students and are invariably poorly answered. Part of the reason is of course that monetary theory is inherently difficult but another reason is the profusion of financial institutions (intermediaries), the complicated relationships between them and the government's apparent keeness for regularly changing both rules the rules and the instruments of monetary control. For example since 1971 we have seen the introduction and effective abandonment of Competition and Credit Control (C.C.C.). With C.C.C. itself we have seen Bank Rate disappear to be replaced by a market determined Minimum Lending Rate (MLR); this in turn we have seen revert to an administered rate before finally being suspended in 1981. Supplementary special deposits have come and gone; monetary targets have been introduced and have been varied from single measures such as M3 to multiple measures such as M1, £M3 and PSL2.

Contrary to students' suspicions this is not clear evidence of ad-hocery or perverseness on the part of the government and the monetary authorities aimed solely at making students' lives difficult, rather it is evidence of the difficulty the policy-makers themselves are having in identifying, measuring and controlling key relationships. Indeed, to complicate things further, important institutional changes have been taking place. For example, the banks have moved into the traditional building society market of house loans and building societies in their turn are now introducing credit cards and chequeing facilities; these changes have serious implications for the measurement of the money supply and underline the policy-makers' problems.

The overall result however does amount to a monetary maze to which too many students feel disinclined to invest valuable resources like time and effort in tracing through.

My objectives in this pamphlet are to provide a short perspective of the role of money in the British economy and to trace through the main developments in the gradual adoption and practice of 'monetarism'.

CHAPTER 1   THE THEORY OF MONEY DEMAND

The economic policy stance of UK governments since 1979 is widely described as 'Monetarist'. This seems to imply that the economic policy stance of governments before 1979 was different in some way - i.e. non-monetarist. Certainly the presumption exists today that money is important and control of its quantity vital if we are to have stability in the price level and through that an economic environment conducive to the achieving of full employment and economic growth.

In this chapter I want to look at the meaning of the terms Monetarist and Non-Monetarist in respect of their theoretical antecedents.

The Demand for Money

A key concept which it is well to deal with at the outset is that of the 'demand for money'. It is my experience that many students never understand its meaning. Put very simply if we have to speak of any individual's demand for money we would be describing the proportion of his total wealth he had decided to hold in those assets we conventionally describe as money (notes, coins and bank deposits) as opposed to all those other assets not so described (shares, gilt-edged securities and property for example). If you as an individual were to realise (sell) all your assets, physical and financial, and turn them into money you would be left with a maximum amount of money that you could hold; we call this your budget constraint. Clearly it would be very inconvenient to hold all your wealth in this way (misers may try to) and you would not do it, nevertheless the amount you do demand to hold is ultimately limited in this way. It is very important for governments to know what factors influence your decision about how much money you actually decide to hold because they are then in a position to predict the results of, for example, an increase in the quantity of money.

This is why of course, so many different economists have theorised about the demand for money and why, before we can proceed any further, we must look at the development of money demand theory. When we have done that we can look at what each theory predicts will happen if there is an increase in the money supply.

The Quantity Theory of Money

The best known expression of the role of money is to be found in the Old Quantity Theory truism:

$MV = PT$ where M = the quantity of money
V = the number of times it turns over, its transactions velocity

P = the price level
T = the volume of transactions

If we assume V and T to be constants we can rewrite this as

$$M\bar{V} = P\bar{T}$$

and then rearrange it to derive both a theory of the demand for money and a theory of the determination of the price level. Thus on the assumption that in equilibrium the supply of money equals the demand for money (Ms = Md) we can substitute Md for M in the equation and rewrite it as:

(1) $$M_d = \frac{1}{\bar{V}} P\bar{T}$$

a theory of the demand for money that states that the demand for money is inversely proportional to its velocity and directly proportional to the total level of activity in the economy ($\bar{T}$) and

(2) $$P = \frac{M\bar{V}}{\bar{T}}$$

a theory of the price level that states that on the assumption that V and T are constants then the price level is determined by, and is proportional to, the quantity of money.

This version of the Old Quantity Theory, associated with Fisher, was very much a Transactions theory, that is to say it emphasised the medium of exchange role of money in the economy. Economists in this tradition wanted to know how much people would have to hold to sustain a particular level of economic activity; it was to that extent a very mechanistic approach to the role of money.

A subsequent version of the theory called the Cambridge Cash Balance theory recognised that money had other functions than as a medium of exchange. Economists in this tradition or variant of the Quantity theory therefore began to ask the question 'how much money do people want to hold and what would cause them to vary their holdings, rather than how much money do people have to hold. Implicit in this, of course, is the idea that V is not fixed as had been assumed. What factors might cause people to alter their money holdings, economising upon them in some periods, holding excess amounts in other periods? The Cambridge theorists suggested, amongst other things, that interest rates and people's expectations about the future were probably important; thus, for example, if interest rates were high then the opportunity cost of holding money would be high (lost interest income) and people would economise on money holdings. The Cambridge theorists did not formally measure the effects of these factors on money demand largely because the statistical data was not available and an understanding of the determination of people's expectations was even less well understood than today. Their change of emphasis however from 'have to hold' to 'want to hold', their recognition that money had other roles than as a medium of exchange found expression in a modified form of the Quantity theory:

(3) $M_d = kY$ where k is a factor of proportionality equivalent to V but no longer fixed.

The equation does not look much different from the Fisher version of the Quantity Theory but it is radically different in its implications and is the direct antecedent of both Keynesian and Modern Monetarist money-demand theory.

<u>Keynesian Money Demand Theory</u>

Keynes was brought up in the Cambridge tradition and it is not surprising therefore that in the development of his own demand for money theory he placed emphasis on 'want to hold'. To this end he concentrated upon peoples 'motives' for wanting to hold money. I don't intend to discuss these at length here although they will be referred to again later. Suffice it to say that Keynes' Transactions and Precautionary motives for holding money fall squarely within the tradition of the Fisher Old Quantity theory and relate the demand to income. His speculative money demand is the major departure and is the explicit development of that which is implicit in the Cambridge 'k'. He argues that some part of people's money holdings will be influenced by interest rates (the opportunity cost of holding money) such that when interest rates are high people will economise on these balances, when interest rates are low they will have little incentive to economise on them. The individual makes his own decision about what is a high or low rate of interest by comparing ruling market rates with his own perception of what they should be, his view of the 'normal rate'.

The Keynesian money demand function is therefore:

Total money demand = Transactions demand + Precautionary demand
                              + Speculative demand

In empirical work it is virtually impossible to distinguish between Transactions and Precautionary balances and it is easier to take them together.

Transactions and Precautionary demand are directly related to income:

i.e. $M_{Tr} = fY$

- 3 -

Speculative demand is related to the rate of interest:
i.e. MSp = fr

(4)   Thus Md = f(Y, r)

A most important point to note here is that the 'r' in the equation relates to the rate of return on financial assets: for Keynesians the alternative to holding money is to hold a small range of well defined financial assets.[1] ie rate of return on a fixed interest government bond.
This point needs to be particularly stressed because what represents an alternative to holding money is a fundamental difference between Keynesian and Modern Monetarist (Friedman) theory.

Modern Monetarist Money Demand Theory

Friedman's theory of money demand is also a linear descendent of the Cambridge Cash Balance theory. Friedman accepts that people's demand for money will be related to their income and he also accepts that their demand for money at any income level will be influenced by such variables as interest rates, expectations about the future, movements in the price level and so on.

Where he differs from Keynes is that he doesn't consider it necessary to elaborate a special theory of money demand (e.g. in terms of motives for wanting to hold money) rather he argues that the demand for money can be analysed perfectly well within the framework of traditional demand theory. People, he argues, will demand money for the same reason that they demand any commodity, that is for the service, the utility, that it yields. The particular service that money yields is that 'it is a ready source of purchasing power'. People will demand more money only in so far as the marginal utility associated with additional increments of 'ready purchasing power' is greater than the marginal utility to be derived from holding more of other assets of all kinds. Money then is not perceived as being different from other assets.

In traditional demand theory the demand for any commodity is expressed as a function of a number of variables. In general this demand function is written as:

q_n^d = f (Pn, P1.....Pn-1, Y, E)

where q_n^d = demand for any commodity n
Pn = price of the commodity n
Y = the income of the individual
Pn...Pn-1 = the price of all other commodities
E = a host of sociological factors (Lipsey 1983)

A demand function such as this is a general formula, it is not meant to be applied to the demand for any particular commodity as though it were a blueprint. What it says, what it emphasises, is that the demand for any commodity, the amount of any commodity that an individual will want to hold, is determined by the individual's budget constraint and the opportunity cost, that is what has to be given up. In actually applying the theory to the demand for any commodity be it second-hand cars, fish, houses or money you must examine the special features of the market for the commodity to identify the appropriate variables to go into the function the emphasis being upon the budget constraint and the appropriate opportunity costs. For example, if you were analysing the demand for houses to buy (as opposed to rent) you would include the income of would-be-purchasers, the rate of interest on mortgages, the price of houses and the availability or otherwise of mortgages. This latter variable would not have been included as a result of examining the general demand formula but its importance is clear when you examine the institutional features of the market for houses to buy.

Friedman postulated such a demand function for money:

(5) $\quad M_d = f(W, r - \frac{1}{r}\frac{dr}{dt}, \frac{1}{P}\frac{dP}{dt}, h) P$

This looks complicated but in effect all that it says is that the demand for money is determined by:

(i) W, that is people's wealth; this is a broader concept than income and does seem appropriate as the ultimate budget constraint.

(ii) $r - \frac{1}{r}\frac{dr}{dt}$ this is a term included to measure the opportunity cost of holding money. It refers to the rate of return on assets alternative to money and to the rate of change of that return. There are a large number of such alternative assets that yield such a rate of return for example bonds, equities and durable goods but on the assumption that rates of return all move together and in the same direction we can simplify the equation enormously by picking one representative rate and letting it stand for all the others.

(iii) $\frac{1}{P}\frac{dP}{dt}$ is the expression that captures the effect on money demand of expected changes in the price level. Given that when the price level changes the value or purchasing power of money changes it is clear that there will be a cost to holding money in inflationary periods. Generally speaking it is not unreasonable to say that the greater the expected change in the price level upwards the less in aggregate will be the demand for money to hold.

(iv) P. Because money is held for the services it performs we must also include the price level itself in our equation.

The higher the price level the greater the demand for money to sustain a particular level of expenditure. If we multiply the whole equation by P, the price level, we can capture this effect.

(v) h. Not only does Friedman widen the budget constraint from Income to Wealth but he refines the concept of wealth to include non-human and human wealth. Non-human wealth accords with the general view of wealth and includes all physical and financial assets; human wealth refers to the endowments of health, education and training possessed differentially by individuals and giving rise to income streams.
The assumption is that the greater the proportion of non-human wealth in an individual's overall wealth the greater his demand for money, the reason being that whereas there are ready markets where you can turn non-human wealth into money there are few such ways of transforming human capital into money. Because in practice it is difficult, if not impossible, to differentiate these component parts of wealth it is assumed that the ratio of human to non-human wealth will not change except in the long term; it is this ratio that is described by the term 'h' in the equation.

The differences between the Keynesian and Modern Monetarist demand-for-money equations can be summarised:

(i) Keynes elaborates a special theory of money demand which concentrates on peoples motives for holding money.

Friedman rejects this approach and analyses the demand for money within the general framework of established demand theory.

(ii) In the money demand equation Keynes uses Income as the determinant of transactions and precautionary money demand.

Friedman goes further and uses Wealth; he also distinguishes between human and non-human wealth. His budget constraint is thus much more all-embracing.

(iii) The rate of return 'r' in the Keynesian analysis is a rate selected to stand as a proxy for rates on financial assets, the alternatives to holding money.

The rate of return 'r' in Friedman's equation is a proxy for the rate of return on all assets, durable consumer goods and financial assets. The opportunity cost of holding money is thus much more widely defined. Not only that but Friedman's equation takes account of the rate of change of rates of return.

(iv) The Keynesian money-demand equation says nothing about the price level or its rate of change.

Friedman's equation sees the expected rate of change of the price level as a relevant opportunity cost; the level of prices is also a relevant variable.

CHAPTER 2   THE MONEY TRANSMISSIONS MECHANISM

We have now looked at the main differences between the Keynesian and Monetarist money demand equations. What implications for policy can be derived from them? Perhaps the easiest way to understand this is by postulating a change in the money supply (as yet undefined but assumed to be within the control of the monetary authority) and by then examining how people, according to the different theories, react to the change. The money transmissions mechanism describes how a change in the money supply works its way through the economy by its effect on decisions to spend.

Let us assume that the monetary authorities want to bring about an increase in the money supply and they do this using open market operations, that is open market purchases of bonds from the non-bank public. What will be the effect of this? The effect will be that the non-bank public will give up bonds and acquire money, they will receive cheques from the Bank of England which they will pay into their bank accounts. What has happened is that in their portfolios, the overall distribution of their wealth, the non-bank public has substituted bank deposits (defined to be money) for bonds (not defined as money), the money supply has thus been increased. The essential difference between Keynesian and Monetarist theory is concerned with what the non-bank public does with these enhanced money balances. And, of course, what they do is explained by the demand-for-money theories. Let us take the Keynesian and Monetarist theories in turn and trace through the portfolio adjustment process after the enhanced money balances have accrued.

Keynesian transmissions mechanism - according to Keynesian theory the non-bank public will try to re-establish portfolio equilibrium (after selling bonds) by using the enhanced money balances to buy the closest substitutes for money, financial assets. This will have the effect of bidding up the prices of those assets and of reducing the yield upon them, the rate of interest. The initial impact will be on short-term rates but there will be a knock-on effect in all financial markets until long-term prices and yields are affected too. "The effect of a change in the money supply is seen to be like a ripple passing along the range of financial assets, diminishing in amplitude and predictability as it proceeds further away from the initial disturbance. This 'ripple' eventually reaches to the long-end of the market causing a change in yields which will bring about a divergence between the cost of capital and the return on capital." (Goodhart, C.A.) (1972).

The effect of changes in the money supply upon expenditure decisions is thus regarded by Keynesians "as taking place almost entirely by way of changes in interest rates on financial assets

- 7 -

caused by the monetary disturbance." (Goodhart op cit). The change in yields at the long end of the markets will stimulate investment expenditures and these with their multiplier and accelerator effects will bring about a change in the level of output and employment.

The Keynesian transmissions mechanism may be depicted as:

$$\Delta M \uparrow \longrightarrow \Delta r \downarrow \longrightarrow \Delta I \uparrow \longrightarrow \Delta GNP \uparrow$$

Empirical work on the relationships depicted above indicated that:

(i) a ΔM seemed to have a small and unpredictable effect upon rates of interest;

(ii) that investment decisions were not very responsive to changes in rates of interest.

With these key relationships seeming to be weak and ineffective it is not surprising that Keynesians decided that if they were to influence expenditures in the economy and thus output and employment, it would be better to do it directly rather than indirectly and very uncertainly through changes in the money supply working on interest rates. This is the reason why postwar governments in the Keynesian tradition have employed active interventionary Fiscal policy and rather neglected Monetary policy and why Keynesians are often referred to as Fiscalists.

<u>Monetarist transmissions mechanism</u> - according to Monetarist theory all goods are perceived as substitutes for money. An individual with enhanced money balances will, according to this theory, re-establish portfolio equilibrium by expanding across the whole range of assets that yield a return. For the monetarist any good that isn't immediately consumed (durable goods) will yield a flow of services over time; this flow of services from, say, a durable good is its 'own-rate' of return and equivalent to the rate of return on financial assets. The fact that it is intangible doesn't make it any the less real. "Keynesians and monetarists agree that asset holders will strive to reach an equilibrium where the services yielded by a stock of money (convenience, liquidity etc) are at the margin equal to the own-rate of interest on other assets. Keynesians by and large believe that the relevant own-rate is that on some financial assets, monetarists that it is the generality of own-rates on all other assets. Keynesians, therefore, expect people to buy financial assets when they feel that they have larger money balances than they strictly require .... whereas monetarists expect the adjustment to take place through 'direct' purchases of a wider range of assets including physical assets such as consumer durables". (Goodhart op cit).

Thus according to the monetarist view the impact of monetary policy will be to cause a small but pervasive change on all planned expenditures whether on goods or financial assets. The impact of changes in the quantity of money will be widely spread rather than working through changes in particular interest rates. The monetarist transmissions mechanism may therefore be depicted as:

$$\Delta M \uparrow \longrightarrow \Delta GNP \uparrow$$

This indicates a very important role for money and thus for monetary policy.

To reinforce these points let us also look at what would happen according to the two theories of money demand if the monetary authorities were to reduce the quantity of money. This could be done by open market sales of government debt.

According to the Keynesian analysis interest rates would be forced up by the sale of bonds; they wouldn't rise by much because any increase in the rates on financial assets which are seen as close substitutes for money would make people prepared to organise their affairs with smaller money balances. Because expenditure decisions are affected indirectly, that is by the rate of interest change rather than directly by the quantity of money change, there would be little reason to expect much of a reduction in spending. The rate of interest change is small and expenditures generally are thought to be interest-rate insensitive anyway, thus the money supply is reduced with little or no impact on spending.

The Monetarist would agree that rates of interest on financial assets would rise as a result of the open market sales. He would not agree, however, that equilibrium would be restored by people being willing to manage their affairs on smaller money balances. Financial asset prices would have fallen and people as a result would want to hold more of them, but they wouldn't hold more of them by deciding to hold smaller money balances, rather they would hold less of all other goods. However "which expenditures would be cut back would depend on the response to the changing pattern, overall, of prices (yields) on the whole range of assets set in motion by the initial monetary disturbance." (Goodhart op cit).

CHAPTER 3   BUT WHAT IS MONEY?

Now it is all very well to derive from theory a role for the money supply but it is altogether a more difficult problem to translate this into policy. If you decide, for example, that control of the money supply is important in managing the economy you can only do that if you know precisely what 'money' is. This typifies a major problem in the social sciences: elaborating 'operational' definitions, that is definitions that are measurable. In fact there is no single unambiguous measure of the money supply; indeed since the Budget of 1982 we have had official targets for four different measures: M0, M1, Sterling M3 (£M3) and Private Sector Liquidity (PSL). As well as this we have measured and monitored M2 and M3. (See page 13 for definitions of these).

In the UK today there exists a wide diversity of assets in which any individual can hold his wealth. Most individuals, for example, will have some notes and coins, a large number will have a bank deposit, an even greater number perhaps will have a building society deposit or a national savings account; increasing numbers of people own shares in companies and have insurance policies. And, of course, we don't only hold our wealth in these various financial assets, we hold physical assets too: houses and land for example. The collection of assets in which any individual holds his wealth (and we all hold different collections) is referred to as we have seen as his PORTFOLIO. The question is which of these assets are perceived by their owners as money? When we want a measure of the money supply, in other words, which assets do we look to?

The best way to proceed here is to rank all assets in order of liquidity where we measure liquidity in terms of:

(a) the ease with which an asset can be converted into spending on goods and services, and

(b) the certainty that the capital value of the asset will be maintained after conversion.

Thus cash (notes and coin) is the most liquid asset in the UK economy because it is automatically acceptable in virtually all transactions; a share in a quoted company on the other hand is a very illiquid asset because it is not acceptable in exchange, it takes time to sell it, you must pay a premium to those who sell it for you and because share prices vary daily you may make a loss if you have to sell it suddenly. Clearly there can be a significant difference in liquidity between assets. To illustrate this further let us list some of the most common classes of assets in decreasing order of liquidity:

Asset

Liquid ↓   Cash - notes and coins
               Current Accounts at banks
               Deposit Accounts at banks
               Building Society deposits
               National Savings deposits

               Shares in quoted companies
               Gilt-edged securities
               Insurance policies
Illiquid ↑   Houses

We apply the term 'money' to those assets that fulfil the functions of money. The difficulty is that we cannot differentiate sharply between assets that are next to each other in the liquidity spectrum and, of course, some assets perform more than one money function. The result is that we cannot unambiguously define money. For example, M0 is the narrowest definition of money that we have; it unambiguously measures spending power in that it is composed almost entirely of notes and coins, the most liquid of all assets and used exclusively as a medium of exchange.

The measure M1 is slightly wider and includes current accounts; cheques drawn on current accounts perform the greatest value (as opposed to number) of exchanges and current accounts are evidently seen by their owner as a 'ready source of purchasing power', a medium of exchange. What then of deposit accounts? They are not as liquid as current accounts theoreticaly because you are supposed to give seven days notice before withdrawing them, although in practice many people do overdraw their current accounts and then transfer deposit accounts; in other words many people use their deposit accounts as transactions balances. It follows that if we are looking for a measure of spending power in the economy, a measure of money, then we cannot ignore bank deposit accounts. The monetary authorities accept this and M3 measures the sum total of notes, coins, current accounts and deposit accounts in existence. This is a relatively wide measure of spending power or the money supply, but it isn't the widest. The reasons that I have given above for including such financial assets as current and deposit accounts in the measure of money is equally validly extended to certain building society and national savings deposits. For example, many people still do not have bank accounts and accordingly treat their building society deposits as a medium of exchange. The building societies have recognised this and some have quite recently introduced credit cards and chequeing facilities that will allow their customers to draw on their deposits in the same way that a depositor with a bank does. It follows that if people are treating their building society and national savings deposits as spending power then not to include those deposits in the monetary measure is to understate it. We have a measure of money that does include these deposits, it is called Private Sector Liquidity (PSL) and is the widest measure of the money supply currently in use.

It must be stressed that no one definition is right, there is no unambiguous definition of the money supply. The UK monetary authorities accept this and today characteristically target more than one measure. (See Chapter 7, page 33).

Thus in the Budget of 1982 it was announced that official targets were to exist for the monetary measures M1, Sterling M3 and PSL2. In the Budget of 1984 it was announced that these would be replaced by one narrow measure M0 (the monetary base) and one wide measure, Sterling M3, where 'narrow money' refers generally to money held predominantly for spending immediately or in the near future on goods and services, i.e. for transactions purposes, and 'broad money' refers generally to money held for transactions purposes and as a store of value: it provides an indicator of the private sector's holdings of relatively liquid assets in other words.

The relationships between the different measures of money can be seen in the Table overleaf.

- 12 -

RELATIONSHIPS AMONG THE MONETARY AND LIQUIDITY AGGREGATES AND THEIR COMPONENTS

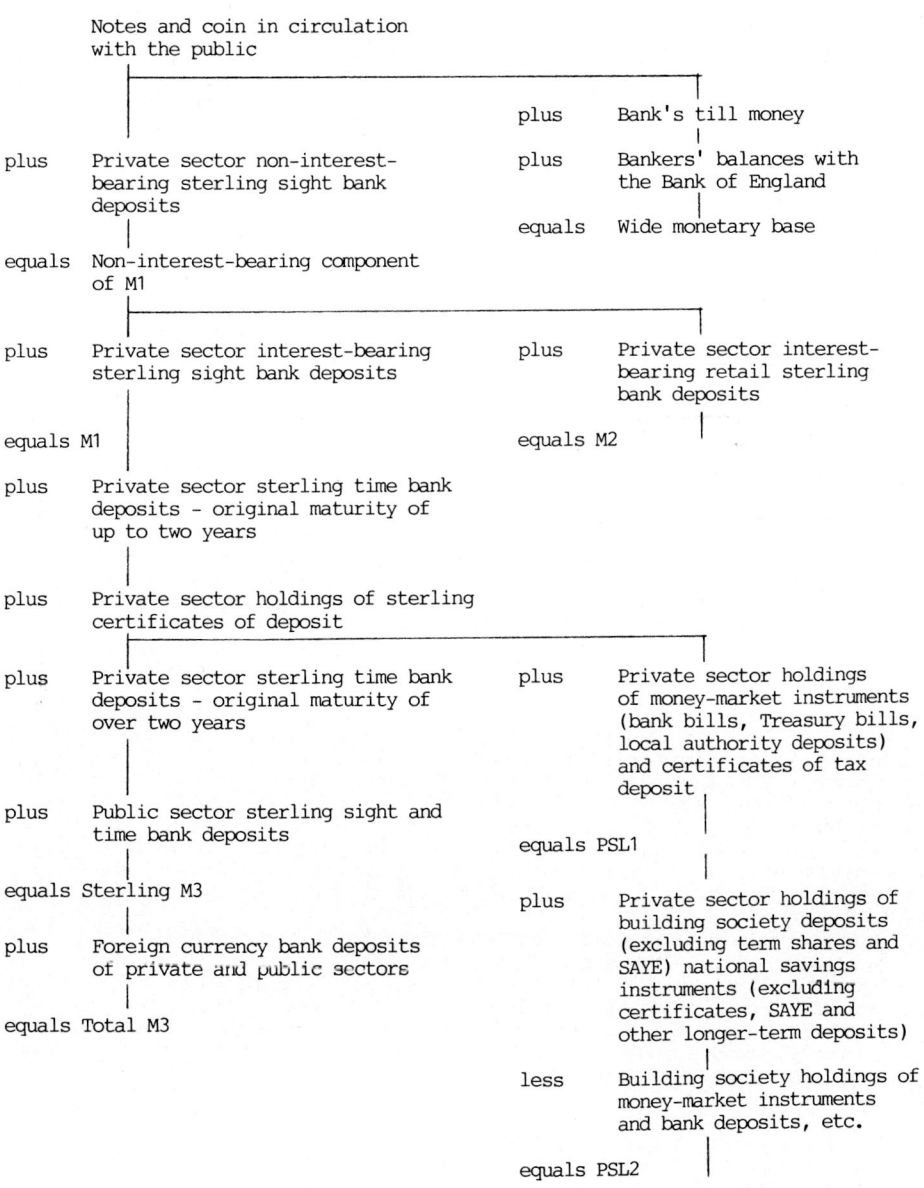

Source: Bank of England Quarterly Bulletin

CHAPTER 4   THE ADOPTION OF THE MONETARIST PHILOSOPHY IN THE UK

C.E.J.Dennis (1982) argues that the debate on the role of the money supply in UK macro-economic policy really began in the UK with the Letter of Intent sent to the IMF immediately after the devaluation of sterling in 1967. The Letter contained the first mention of money supply targets for the UK promising to keep money supply growth in 1968 in line with its growth in 1967. A second Letter was sent in May 1969 setting a limit for DCE (Domestic Credit Expansion) of £400m for 1969-70.

The practice of announcing a monetary target for DCE ceased in 1971 - this was partly due to the strength of sterling but also due to the authorities' confidence that control of the money supply could be facilitated through its Competition and Credit Control (CCC) techniques introduced in that year. (See page 19 and Appendix 1). The cartel on interest rates was abandoned in the CCC framework as were direct controls on bank lending; control was to be implemented through transactions in a defined range of liquid reserve assets. At the same time, as the introduction of CCC another significant change took place that emphasised the authorities' new approach both to competition in financial markets and to a role for money in macroeconomic policy: the authorities ceased to support gilt prices and began to tolerate small variations, with complete support of the market at one price being abandoned. The fostering of orderly conditions in the market for government debt was a central theme of policy during the 1950's and 1960's and was illustrative of the low importance attached to the money supply - the shift in policy at the end of the 1960's was a very important indicator of a change in the official view to an acceptance that money was no longer to be considered unimportant.

The steady conversion in the 1970's to a belief in a positive role for money was marked by a continuing debate on the role of money in academic circles as well as in speeches by the Chancellor and the Governor of the Bank of England. The Conservative government of the early 1970's adopted a policy stance which clearly recognised a role for money whilst not accepting or believing the full monetarist implications of that stance - indeed the money supply grew so rapidly in the two years following September 1971 that restrictions on bank lending had to be reimposed.

The formal introduction of £M3 targets introduced in late 1976 as part of an IMF support package following the sterling crisis of that year marks the broad acceptance of monetarist thinking in official policy-making but serious evidence that the new approach to monetary policy had been widely adopted is perhaps most clearly demonstrated in the widely quoted statement of Prime Minister James Callaghan in 1976:

"We used to think that you could spend your way out of a recession, and increase employment, by cutting taxes and boosting government spending. I tell you in all candour that that option no longer exists and that in so far as it ever did exist it worked by injecting inflation into the economy. And each time that happened the average level of unemployment has risen. Higher inflation followed by higher unemployment. That is the history of the last 20 years."

The Conservative government elected in 1979 brought the process to an end. It appeared to have adopted wholeheartedly the monetarist doctrine as the basis of its macroeconomic policy.

How do we account for this gradual adoption of a more important role for money? Two important reasons or groups of reasons can be pointed to:

(i) Accumulating evidence on the role of monetary factors in the determination of nominal income - in particular empirical work on:

- money multipliers

- demand for money studies

- correlation studies of time series of money and economic activity.

In particular there was much evidence by 1970 that in the UK money demand was a stable function of a few variables and this did lead to considerable attention being given to control of the money supply as an instrument of policy.[2]

(ii) The alleged failure of demand-management policies: the fine-tuning of the Keynesian tradition. The unpredictable lags involved in identifying problems and then selecting and implementing appropriate policy responses to them was felt to have aggravated as much as moderated problems. The collapse of the Phillips Curve and the development of stagflation marked the beginning of the end of detailed discretionary intervention in the economy and the beginning of the adoption of the formal monetarist approach (completed in 1979) - fixed, global rules embodied in a medium or long-run strategy.

What then is this monetarist philosophy embraced by the Conservative government of 1979? What are its main features?

As Laidler (1981) writes "like beauty, 'monetarism' tends to lie in the eye of the beholder and before it can be assessed it must be defined."[3] In his view the key characteristics of monetarism are:

1. A quantity theory approach to macroeconomic analysis in two distinct senses: (a) that used by Milton Friedman (1956)

to describe a theory of the demand for money and (b) the more traditional sense of a view that fluctuations in the quantity of money are the dominant cause of fluctuations in money income.

2. The analysis of the division of money income fluctuations between the price level and real income in terms of an expectations augmented Phillips curve whose structure rules out an economically significant long-run inverse trade-off between the variables.

3. A monetary approach to balance-of-payments and exchange-rate theory.

4. (a) Antipathy to activist stabilisation policy, either monetary or fiscal, and to wage and price controls, and (b) support for long-run monetary policy 'rules' or at least prestated 'targets', cast in terms of the behaviour of some monetary aggregate rather than of the level of interest rates.

1. Categorises the theoretical core of monetarism as it developed in the 1950's and 1960's the essential features of which I have discussed in Chapter 1 above. 2. and 3. represent theory developed or absorbed by monetarists since the mid 1960's. While 4. summarises a view of macroeconomic policy issues which, ... has remained reasonably constant among monetarists for the last quarter century.

Monetarists have been clear that an increase in the money stock will raise nominal income (GNP). They have not been clear until quite recently about the division of the effect of any change in the money stock between prices and real income. Monetarists now reject the notion that monetary policy will have a permanent effect on real output but do believe that short-run effects are possible. It seemed the case that a change in the money stock would lead to a change in output after a six to nine months lag with prices affected after a further six to nine months. Laidler (1981 op cit) now argues that this lagged effect on output and then prices can be theoretically explained by the Expectations Augmented Phillips' curve (See Appendix 2) - the 'missing equation of the monetarist model' as he calls it: the change in the money stock leads to a change in output and employment until inflation is fully anticipated whereupon output and employment return to the natural level. Most importantly there is no long-run trade-off as in the traditional Phillips curve. "The vertical long-run Phillips curve at the natural level of unemployment is not now a distinctive aspect of monetarism as it is more widely accepted and supported by empirical evidence". (Purvis, P.D. 1980)

This major prediction of the monetarist model was adopted by the

Conservative government elected in 1979 and underpins its Medium Term Financial Strategy (MTFS) within which global rules are adopted both for the money stock (target aggregate(s)) and government spending and revenue raising (summarised in a target for the Public Sector Borrowing Requirement (PSBR)).

Although the expectations-augmented Phillips curve explained the breakdown between output and price effects of a change in the money stock it said nothing about the speed of the adjustment process - how long it would take the economy to reach long-run equilibrium. Given that the real effects (on output and employment) were short run and confined to a period when expectations were unfulfilled the question was concerned with what determines expectations? An answer was provided by the Rational Expectations Hypothesis (REH).[4] This hypothesis had led to a questioning of whether a short-run period of real effect would be experienced at all. The approach predicts that except for random shocks all policy development will be perfectly anticipated so that any inflationary expectations will be influenced immediately and monetary policy will have no real effects. The prediction has become known as the "irrelevance hypothesis" after Brunner (1981).

It seems now that the Conservative government of 1979 embraced this hypothesis too - the announcement of its 'credible targets' in the MTFS of 1980 seems to bear witness to this. It must however be said that the objective of a gradual reduction of inflation evidenced in the slowly reducing MTFS targets indicates some scepticism.

In the early 1980's the fact that the size of wage settlements began to decline was quoted in support of the REH although it now seems more likely that this was the result of high unemployment resulting from, amongst other things, high exchange rates.

Nevertheless the announcement of the MTFS may have been needed to give credibility to a long-run monetary policy, notwithstanding the implications of a naive version of REH. The Bank of England clearly takes this view when they write "we have come to distinguish rather sharply between the 'political economy' of a money supply strategy and the practical economics of a money supply policy. The former has to do with political presentation to a wide variety of audiences that constitute the public and whose perceptions of the strategy presented is very diverse .... 'practical macroeconomics' is concerned with macroeconomic relationships and their stability or instability". (J.S.Fforde 1983)

Given the acceptance by the Conservative government of the central policy recommendations of monetarism:

(i)   a monetary rule with the rate of growth of the money stock set independently of economic conditions and

(ii) the rejection of demand-management stabilisation policies it was then necessary to consider conditions for effecting them.

This required elaborating:

(i) Adequate concepts and techniques of measurement for the relevant monetary aggregate(s) (See Chapter 3).

(ii) Institutional arrangements facilitating control of the monetary aggregate(s).

(iii) Well designed internal procedures to implement such controls.[5]

In the next chapter I want to look at the arrangements for monetary control that were introduced in August 1981 and which still apply at the time of writing in mid-1984.

CHAPTER 5   THE OPERATION OF MONETARY CONTROL IN THE UK

In this Chapter I want to examine the institutional framework within which control of the money supply by interest-rate manipulation is effected.

What are the methods of monetary control?

The three main weapons now employed in the United Kingdom are fiscal policy, debt management (or funding) and changes in short-term interest rates. (Davies, A. 1984).

Fiscal policy is concerned with the government's effort to control and lower the PSBR as this is of itself a direct counterpart to changes in the sterling M3 measure of the money supply. The problem is that in the short-term the PSBR is difficult to control. Nevertheless downward pressure on the PSBR is seen as a major plank of money supply control over the medium term.

Sales of most forms of public sector debt to the non-bank private sector represent a key instrument in restraining monetary growth. Gilt-edged funding remains the dominant instrument but National Savings have assumed increased importance in recent years. Funding is essentially the means whereby the monetary authorities seek to neutralise the expansionary effects on the money supply of the PSBR.[6] On occasions sales of debt have substantially exceeded the PSBR (a practice known as 'over funding') in order to offset strong bank lending growth. Thus in 1981/82 sales of public sector debt to the non-bank UK private sector exceeded £11 billion compared to a PSBR in that year of less than £9 billion.

Whereas control of the PSBR and funding are directed in a fairly explicit way at controlling the money supply the rationale for changes in short-term interest rates is that through them the demand for bank loans can be influenced and thus the money supply.

Most of the remainder of this chapter will look at the way in which short-term interest rates are currently controlled by the Bank of England by its operations in the money markets and principally through its dealings with the discount houses and transactions in commercial bills. But before that is done it is necessary to look briefly at the arrangements for monetary control before 1981.

Development of Competition in the UK Banking System

Throughout the 1950's and 1960's the UK banking system was subjected to continuous quantitative restrictions that were harmful to its competitive position vis a vis other financial intermediaries. It has been argued that the term 'financial repression' would be an appropriate description of the financial regime of that time. It is a term that describes how government interference with interest rates and credit allocation can hamper economic growth by reducing total investment and directing the investment which does take place to the wrong places.

Given the restrictions on the banking system in general it is not surprising that the demand for credit was increasingly met by other financial institutions. Finance houses provided the credit for consumer durable expenditure; Building Societies for private house purchases; the Capital market provided medium-term finance to companies for investment through new debenture issues. The 1950's and 1960's was a period when the banks steadily lost ground to each of these intermediaries.

The introduction of the Competition and Credit Control reforms of 1971 (Appendix 1) were a recognition of the distortions that had developed and a response to a clamour from bankers and academic economists for change. All restrictions on bank lending were abolished in an effort to put banks and non-banks on a more equal footing in the struggle to capture an increased share of financial intermediation. The immediate result was a doubling of bank lending to the private sector (in the two years from September 1971). In December 1974 the authorities, thoroughly alarmed, introduced Supplementary Special Deposits (the Corset) - a reversion to direct quantitative restriction. Its essential aim was to check the expansion of bank lending - the experiment seemed to be over.

From 1974 to 1980 the banks continued to be subject to limitations on their lending activity. The Corset is perhaps the best known of these limitations, being invoked on three separate occasions; in all it was in operation for half of the period December 1973 to June 1980 when it was abolished. In addition to the Corset however, there were qualitative guidelines discouraging credit to the personal sector which did much to further encourage the growth of the Finance Houses and particularly the Building Societies relative to the banks. In addition to these factors the banks also had to bear the costs of the reserve asset ratio which obliged them to keep a minimum of $12\frac{1}{2}\%$ of their eligible liabilities in specified liquid assets where the rate of return was relatively low. As with other companies they suffered from exchange control which prevented them from lending in sterling overseas.

Since 1979 all these regulations have been scrapped. The Corset was withdrawn in June 1980 leaving the banks free to develop their corporate lending. In 1981 nearly all restrictions on lending to the personal sector were ended and although no formal announcement was made the banks were given to understand that they could develop mortgage finance business. Exchange controls were abolished in October 1979 allowing sterling lending to foreigners. The reserve asset ratio and the $1\frac{1}{2}\%$ cash ratio also lapsed in 1981.

It is perhaps fair to say that banks in Britain now operate in a freer environment than at any time in the post-war period.

The sequence of liberalisation moves between 1979 and August 1981 represents the second change in the process begun by CCC in September 1971; the overriding motivation was to establish equality of competition between different kinds of financial intermediary after 40 years of distorting interventionism in UK banking, but the process was accelerated by the accession to office of a Conservative Government committed to the Monetarist philosophy and a belief in the efficiency of competitive markets.

The Post-1981 Money Market Structure

The institutional framework within which monetary control has been implemented since August 1981 can be depicted in the following way:

The UK Banking Sector

```
              Bank of England
             Issue Department
    Notes & Coin issued on demand to Banks
```

- Direct Loans
- Bill Markets
- Cash Ratio ½% of eligible liabilities maintained at the Bank of England
- Discount Houses
- Eligibility Requirements 5% secured money ratio of which 2½% is with LDMA
- Eligible Banks
- Other Recognised Banks / Licensed Deposit Takers / Trustee Saving Banks / National Giro
- Money brokers & Gilt Edged Jobbers
- Inter-Bank Market

Legend:
- ▨ New Banking Sector ⎫
- ☐   ⎬ Institutions
- ◯ Flow of Funds

Source: Barclays Bank Review
November 1981

To facilitate the operation of monetary control through this framework some substantial alterations were made to the instruments of CCC. These can be summarised as follows:

(i) Interest Rates

Perhaps the most important change was the suspension of Minimum Lending Rate (MLR) and the introduction of the new methods of interest rate control. The avowed objective of discontinuing MLR was to allow market forces a greater say in the determination of interest rates. The Bank of England now seeks to keep short-term interest rates within an unpublished band, through its bill dealings with the discount houses. The Bank of England may change its views on the range of interest rates from time to time (as it did in September 1981 when it engineered a rise), when it will seek to implement its wishes through its activities in the market. MLR, however, has only been 'put on ice'; it has not been abandoned. The authorities can re-activate it should they wish but, to date, have not done so.

(ii) Acceptable bills

The rules regarding what the Bank of England would recognise as an 'acceptable name' on a bill of exchange were also changed in August 1981. Gone is the requirement that an acceptable bank name has to be British. The list now includes many overseas banks in London, and the extension has given the Bank a wider range of bills which it may use in its money market operations.

(iii) Cash ratio

The reserve assets ratio was abandoned in August 1981, as was the requirement that the clearing banks alone had to keep 1.5% of their eligible liabilities in cash at the Bank of England.

The Bank of England now requires members of the 'monetary sector' whose eligible liabilities exceed £10m to keep 0.5% of their deposits at the Bank of England. The 'monetary sector' includes:

(a) all recognised banks and licensed deposit-takers (LDTs);
(b) National Girobank;
(c) those banks in the Channel Islands and the Isle of Man which opt to join the cash ratio scheme;
(d) the trustee savings banks (TSBs);
(e) the Banking Department of the Bank.

Some redefinition of eligible liabilities has been necessary under the new arrangements. The following can be offset against a bank's liabilities in arriving at its eligible liabilities figure:

(a) funds (other than cash ratio deposits or special deposits placed with the Bank) lent by one institution in the newly defined monetary sector to any other;

(b) money at call placed with money brokers and gilt-edged jobbers in the Stock Exchange, and secured on gilt-edged stocks, Treasury bills, local authority bills and eligible bank bills.

(iv) Undertaking by 'eligible banks'

In 1981, each bank whose bills are recognised as 'eligible' under (ii) above undertook:

(a) that it would maintain 6% of its eligible liabilities on a secured basis, with members of the London Discount Market Association (LDMA) and/or with money brokers and gilt-edged jobbers;

(b) that the proportion held with the LDMA would not fall below 4% of eligible liabilities on any day.

These figures were reduced in 1983 and are now 5% (instead of 6%) and 2.5% (compared with 4%). Full details of this and other minor changes appeared in the September 1983 Bank of England Quarterly Bulletin. Each bank aims to meet the daily average over either a six or 12-month period (the choice of period being notified to the Bank of England). This ratio must not go below the average figure on a daily basis, except in exceptional circumstances, which the bank concerned must justify to the Bank of England.

(v) Liquidity

Although the reserve asset ratio no longer applies, the banks have agreed to discuss in advance with the Bank of England, any change they may be contemplating in their liquidity management and the composition of their liquid assets. In addition, prudential guidelines on liquidity and capital adequacy have been established following the Banking Act 1979.

(vi) Bank of England operations in the gilt-market

The Bank of England now confines its automatic purchases of gilt-edged stock in the market to a maximum of three months to maturity, rather than the pre-1981 one-year-rule.

As a result of the above regulations the authorities have fixed the amounts and types of liquid assets required from the banking community and monetary control techniques revolve around these minimum requirements (points (iii) and (iv) above).

The weekly Treasury bill tender still takes place but the Bank of England no longer tries to generate artificial liquidity shortages to allow it to keep interest rates high, rather it tends to offer only enough Treasury bills to cover the Government's requirements. The essential difference now is that instead of dealing with the discount market at quoted prices the Bank responds to offers from the discount houses. That is when the market requires funds it now offers to sell bills to the Bank. The Bank decides whether the price at which bills are offered (with the implied interest rate) is consistent with its view of where it wants short-term interest rates to be (the undisclosed band). If it is it accepts the offer, if it is not it refuses and the discount houses may have the opportunity to re-offer at a different price (interest rate). Bills bought from the market in this way are quoted in maturity bands, that is in days to maturity. There are four bands in all.

Band 1   bills with up to 14 days to maturity

Band 2   bills with a maturity of between 15 and 33 days

Band 3   bills with a maturity of between 34 and 63 days

Band 4   bills with a maturity of between 64 and 91 days

The abandonment of MLR broke the 'direct' control that the Bank had on the level of short-term interest rates and bank base rates in particular. Since then the Bank has described its operational aim in the money markets as being to keep very short term interest rates within an unpublished band whilst allowing market forces a greater role in determining the structure of interest rates. However, because the Bank still stands ready to supply the banking system with the 'cash' it requires, the rate at which the Bank will supply funds still represents to an extent the marginal cost of funds to the system and acts as a pivot to the structure of interest rates - just as MLR did. It should be stressed here that the Bank does not attempt to control longer term rates to any great extent so that three months inter-bank rates for example will be much more subject to the forces of the market.

The traditional 'lender of last resort' role of the Bank has, of course, been replaced by the present method of relieving cash shortages, but in essence this is only a change in respect of its method of operation and the central role of the discount houses as the buffer between the Bank of England and the commercial banks remains intact.

Having emphasised the three key elements involved in current monetary control technique in the UK let me equally emphasise those techniques _not_ currently in operation. First of all, direct quantitative controls have not been used since the abolition of the 'corset' in 1980 being somewhat discredited because they were so easy to circumvent, especially since the abolition of exchange control. Second, and most important, the monetary authorities do not seek to control the reserves of the banking system with a view to influencing bank lending. The eligible banks are, of course, as we have seen, required to keep a specified volume of funds with the discount houses (and gilt-edged jobbers and money brokers) but the sole purpose of these ratios is to ensure that the discount houses receive sufficient funds to maintain an adequate market in bills. One final point worth making is the extent to which commercial bills dominate the balance sheets of the discount houses. In October 1983 commercial bill holdings were £3.1 billion compared with the discount houses total sterling assets of £6.2 billion. Treasury bill holdings were just £123 million. Other principal assets were Certificates of Deposit (£1.6 billion) and gilt-edged securities (£468 million).

CHAPTER 6   MONEY MARKETS AND THE STRUCTURE OF INTEREST RATES

There are in practice a number of money markets in operation. In the last chapter we discussed how control of the money supply through interest rates was achieved by the Bank of England working in the discount market. The discount market is often referred to as the primary money market because it is the market through which monetary policy is implemented; it is also referred to in some texts as the secured market because loans are 'secured'. The main participants in this market, as we have seen, are the Bank of England, the commercial banks and the discount houses.

But there also exists a series of parallel money markets. In the table on page   these parallel markets are summarised by the term Inter-bank market. This term is often given to the collectivity of parallel markets because the inter-bank market is the largest of them. In fact the parallel money market is composed of a number of discrete markets and includes in order of historical development:

   The Local Authority market;
   The Finance House market;
   The Inter-bank market;
   The Certificate of Deposit market;
   The Company market.

These parallel markets are sometimes referred to as the secondary markets or the unsecured markets. This plethora of names means that students have to be on their guard when reading. The primary and secondary money markets are short-term markets dealing in bills (as opposed to bonds) and short-term deposits.[7]

<u>The Primary Market</u> - we have seen that in the primary market the discount houses use funds borrowed very short-term and largely from the banks in order mainly to discount bills, principally commercial bills, but Treasury bills also.

<u>The Secondary Market</u> - these markets provide liquid assets for the participants and they also provide profitable lending opportunities. They play no direct role in the Bank of England's implementation of monetary policy. To give an example of how they work let us look at the Local Authority Market. A local authority such as Durham County Council, with large and regular outgoings (salaries, taxation payments and purchase of materials) and large receipts (rate payments and rents for example), may find itself on any day with cash balances far in excess of that day's needs. Indeed one of the first jobs of the day for the County Treasurer is to forecast the cash surplus or shortage for that day. If

a surplus is forecast the treasurer will contact one of the many money brokers and attempt to place his surplus at the best rate of interest available. It is the function of the broker to know where shortages of funds exist and thus act to bring lenders and borrowers together. In the local authority market local authorities tend to lend principally to other local authorities and do not make loans to other bodies; in that sense it is a discrete market. In fact Durham County will lend to other local authorities and also to the major clearing banks. It is up to any local authority however, to say to whom it is not willing to lend and the broker will respect that instruction. The Table below gives an indication of the dealings of Durham County Council in early March 1984.

Date of Loan	Borrower	Amount of Loans	Rate of Interest	Period of Notice
24.2.84	Sunderland Metropolitan Borough Council	500,000	9 1/8	2 Days
24.2.84	St Helens Metropolitan Borough Council	300,000	9 1/8	Call
1.3.84	Cynon Valley District Council	250,000	9 1/4	Call
1.3.84	Cunninghame District Council	350,000	9 3/16	Call
2.3.84	Montgomery District Council	250,000	9 1/8	7 Days
2.3.84	Milton Keynes District Council	300,000	9 1/8	2 Days
2.3.84	Southampton City Council	400,000	9 1/8	2 Days
5.3.84	Western Isles Island Council	400,000	9	Call
7.3.84	Lliw Valley District Council	500,000	9 1/8	2 Days
7.3.84	Warrington Borough Council	600,000	9 1/8	2 Days
7.3.84	Guildford Borough Council	250,000	9 1/8	2 Days
7.3.84	Renfrew District Council	350,000	9 1/8	Call
7.3.84	Oxford City Council	300,000	9 1/8	Call
7.3.84	Aberconwy Borough Council	300,000	9 1/8	Call
7.3.84	London Borough of Harrow	400,000	9	Call
9.3.84	Dumbarton District Council	250,000	9 1/8	Call
9.3.84	Mid-Suffolk District Council	250,000	9 1/8	Call
9.3.84	Gordon District Council	200,000	9 1/8	Call
12.3.84	St Albans District Council	150,000	9	Call
14.3.84	London Borough of Camden	1,000,000	8 3/4	Fixed to 29.3.84
14.3.84	Greater London Council	1,000,000	8 3/4	Fixed to 23.3.84

Banks, Finance Houses and Companies operate in much the same way - contacting money brokers to place or borrow surplus funds for short periods of time thus, if they are a lender, maintaining liquidity whilst securing profitable business. The discount houses are now large dealers in Certificates of Deposit.[8]

Money market bill rates and deposit rates for all maturities from overnight to one year are published daily in the Financial Times. The Table below relates to April 26th 1984.

LONDON MONEY RATES — Discount Houses Deposit and Bill Rates

Apr. 26 1984	Sterling Certificate of deposit	Interbank	Local Authority deposits	Company Deposits	Market Deposits	Treasury (Buy)	Treasury (Sell)	Eligible Bank (Buy)	Eligible Bank (Sell)	Fine Trade (Buy)
Overnight	—	$6-9\tfrac{1}{2}$	$8\tfrac{11}{16}-8\tfrac{3}{4}$	$8\tfrac{1}{2}-8\tfrac{3}{4}$	$7-8\tfrac{9}{16}$	—	—	—	—	—
2 days notice	—	—	$8\tfrac{5}{8}$	—	—	—	—	—	—	—
7 days or	—	—	—	—	—	—	—	—	—	—
7 day notice	—	$8\tfrac{1}{2}-8\tfrac{1}{16}$	$8\tfrac{5}{8}$	$8\tfrac{5}{8}-8\tfrac{3}{4}$	$8\tfrac{1}{2}$	—	—	—	—	—
One month	$8\tfrac{5}{8}-8\tfrac{7}{8}$	$8\tfrac{7}{8}-8\tfrac{1}{16}$	$8\tfrac{5}{8}$	$8\tfrac{3}{4}$	$8\tfrac{1}{2}$	$8\tfrac{1}{2}$	$8\tfrac{1}{2}$	$8\tfrac{1}{2}$	$8\tfrac{7}{16}$	$9\tfrac{1}{8}$
Two months	$8\tfrac{3}{4}-8\tfrac{1}{16}$	$8\tfrac{1}{8}-8\tfrac{3}{4}$	$8\tfrac{5}{8}$	$8\tfrac{7}{8}$	$8\tfrac{1}{2}-8\tfrac{3}{4}$	$8\tfrac{1}{16}$	$8\tfrac{7}{16}$	$8\tfrac{1}{2}$	$8\tfrac{7}{16}$	$9\tfrac{1}{32}$
Three months	$8\tfrac{7}{8}-8\tfrac{1}{16}$	$8\tfrac{1}{8}-8\tfrac{1}{16}$	$8\tfrac{1}{2}$	$9\tfrac{1}{8}$	$8\tfrac{1}{2}-8\tfrac{5}{8}$	$8\tfrac{1}{2}$	$8\tfrac{5}{8}$	$8\tfrac{1}{2}$	$8\tfrac{7}{16}$	$9\tfrac{1}{32}$
Six months	$9\tfrac{7}{16}-8\tfrac{1}{16}$	$9\tfrac{1}{16}-9\tfrac{1}{16}$	9	—	—	—	—	$8\tfrac{1}{2}$	$8\tfrac{5}{8}$	—
Nine months	$9\tfrac{1}{4}-9\tfrac{7}{16}$	$9\tfrac{7}{16}-9\tfrac{1}{16}$	$9\tfrac{1}{4}$	—	—	—	—	—	—	—
One year	$9\tfrac{9}{32}-9\tfrac{7}{16}$	$9\tfrac{7}{16}-9\tfrac{1}{2}$	$9\tfrac{5}{8}$	—	—	—	—	—	—	—

Source: Financial Times April 27th 1984

What factors affect the level, structure and pattern of Money Market Interest Rates?

As we already know the Bank controls very short-term rates through its activities in the discount market where it always stands ready to offset shortages or surpluses of funds (the lender of last resort role); to this extent it has control over the marginal cost of funds to the banking system. Its activities are well illustrated by the comment that accompanied the above Table in the Financial Times:

MONEY MARKETS

London rates show little change

UK rates were little changed yesterday despite a weaker pound. Three-month eligible bank bills were bid at $8\tfrac{7}{16}$ per cent, unchanged from Wednesday as was three-month interbank money at $8\tfrac{11}{16}-8\tfrac{5}{8}$ per cent. Overnight interbank money tended to fluctuate a little more however, as the Bank of England absorbed a £600m shortage in four separate operations. Opening rates were quoted at $8\tfrac{1}{2}-8\tfrac{3}{4}$ per cent and rose to 9 per cent before easing back to $8\tfrac{1}{4}$ per cent. Renewed demand then prompted a high of $9\tfrac{1}{4}$ per cent and after drifting away to 6 per cent, closing balances were exchanged at 7-8 per cent.

The Bank forecast a shortage of around £550m initially with factors affecting the market including maturing assistance and a take up of Treasury bills together draining £198m, and Exchequer transactions a further £235m. There was also a rise in the note circulation of £15m and banks brought forward balances £90m below target.

To ease the shortage the Bank offered an early round of assistance which comprised purchases of £17m of eligible bank bills in band 1 (up to 14 days) at $8\tfrac{7}{16}$ per cent and £10m in band 2 (15-33 days) at $8\tfrac{1}{4}$ per cent. In band 3 (34-63 days) it bought £3m of eligible bank bills at $8\tfrac{7}{16}$ per cent and in band 4 (64-91 days) £68m at $8\tfrac{1}{4}$ per cent. The forecast was revised to a shortage of around £600m before taking into account the early help and the market received additional assistance in the morning of £131m. This comprised purchases of £36m of eligible bank bills in band 1 at $8\tfrac{7}{16}$ per cent and £35m in band 2 at $8\tfrac{1}{4}$ per cent. In band 3 it bought £2m of eligible bank bills at $8\tfrac{7}{16}$ per cent and in band 4 £8m of Treasury bills, £3m of local authority bills and £47m of eligible bank bills all at $8\tfrac{1}{4}$ per cent.

Further assistance was given in the afternoon of £248m with purchases of £98m of eligible bank bills in band 1 at $8\tfrac{7}{16}$ per cent and in band 2 £4m of Treasury bills and £36m of eligible bank bills at $8\tfrac{1}{4}$ per cent.

Source: Financial Times April 27th 1984

The bands where the Bank's control is strongest are bands one and two and changes in bill dealing rates in these bands is usually taken to signify that a change in the general level of interest rates is intended. As far as the level of short-term interest rates is concerned then the Bank still exerts an important influence even though the MLR has been suspended.

Market forces have a more important influence on longer term money market rates (Davies, A. 1982). Two forces of great importance here are liquidity preference and market expectations. Generally speaking the longer a loan is the higher the rate of interest will be as investors expect to be compensated for tying funds up for long periods of time. In addition the rate of interest on a one year loan is going to be influenced by expectations of what is going to happen to short-term rates over the year. And these expectations are themselves very much influenced by economic events. If, for example, we have high inflation in the UK and the exchange rate falls, observers may deduce that the Bank will soon want to raise interest rates to defend sterling; this will have the result of raising long-term rates in anticipation of the move.

Thus, whereas the level of interest rates is determined by the activities of the Bank in the discount market the structure of interest rates, the relationship between short-term and long-term rates, is determined by the interaction of liquidity preference factors and expectations about the Bank's bill dealings. Thus, for example, it can be seen from the Table above that the rate of interest on Interbank money increases steadily through the maturities from 7 day to one year deposits; a similar relationship can be seen in Local Authority deposits. With expectations stable long-term rates will usually be higher than short-term rates.

But this still leaves us to explain the pattern of interest rates, the difference in rates on different deposits and financial instruments of the same maturity. It is probable, for example, that the three months' rate on Interbank deposits, Local Authority deposits, Company deposits and Treasury bills will be different on any one day. These differences in pattern will be the result in part at least, of perceived differences in risk with Company deposits typically being seen as riskier than Treasury bills and thus paying a higher rate of interest; they will also be the result of demand and supply conditions in the separate markets, conditions which can vary widely both between markets and within the markets.

What determines Base rates? - the commercial banks have come to rely increasingly on the money markets in recent years. "Of the gross sterling deposits of UK banks totalling around £100 billion at the end of 1981 some 20% represented borrowing between the banks themselves". (Davies 1982 op cit). These are the funds that any individual bank uses to adjust its liquidity position in response to the ebb and flow of other sources of funds; they are interbank funds and they represent the marginal cost of bank deposits to any individual bank.

Changes in base rates have come to be decisions taken in response to changes in the marginal cost of these interbank funds.

But which of the interbank rates is most important in influencing base rates? Is it a short rate such as the 7 day rate or a relatively long rate such as the 3 month rate? The answer is that both have an influence but the 3 month rate is the better measure of the marginal cost of funds to the banks and thus is the more important in determining base rates.

Very short term rates, that is up to 7 days, are of some importance to the banks because of the way our system operates today. In the UK, so-called "blue chip" companies can borrow from the banks at base rate plus 1%. It has not been uncommon when market rates have been greater than 1% over base rate for such customers to borrow from the banks and on-lend in the money markets at a profit. Such a process is colloquially referred to as 'round-tripping', (the technical term for taking such profitable advantage of differences in prices is 'arbitrage'). Needless to say the banks and monetary authorities disapprove of this behaviour because it inflates measures of the money supply.

In fact, however, the 7 day rate is not of such importance to base rates because the practice of 'round-tripping' is not rife and 7 day rates do not represent the best measure of the marginal cost of funds to the banks. The answer is that both the 7 day rate and the 3 month rate both have an influence but the 3 month rate is the better measure of the marginal cost of funds to the banks and thus is the more important in determining base rates.

<u>The Term Structure of Interest Rates</u> - as we have already seen the structure of interest rates refers to the relationship between short-term and long-term rates on similar assets with different terms to maturity. This relationship is commonly depicted by a 'yield curve'.

Again, as we have seen, the key factors in explaining the structure of interest rates are:

(i)   Liquidity preference, which implies that long rates will be higher than short, and

(ii) Expectations about the future level of interest rates. The long-term rate of interest should approximate to the average of expected future short-term interest rates which implies that if long rates are above short rates then short rates are expected to rise and if long rates are below short rates then short rates are expected to fall.

Warren Smith (1974) illustrates in a very simple way how interest rate expectations influence the interest rate structure in the bond market. For a more advanced theoretical consideration, Johnson (1974) and the Bank of England (June 1982) are very useful.

Smith considers three situations:

(i) where the concensus of opinion is that interest rates are going to rise;

(ii) where the concensus is that rates are going to fall;

(iii) where the concensus is that rates are going to remain unchanged.

If (i) prevails we could expect the long-term rate to rise relative to the short-term rate. The question is why? The explanation is that if interest rates are expected to rise lenders will avoid long-term securities because they would expect to suffer capital losses when interest rates rose. Such investors would shift their funds towards shorter term loans and securities. In fact some investors may even sell existing holdings of long term securities in advance of the expected price decline. The result of all this would be a shift in the supply of funds from the long to the short-term market. Borrowers on the other hand would feel that this was a good time to borrow long-term, that is before interest rates rose. As a consequence of the shift of supply from the long to the short-term market and the shift of demand from the short to the long-term market, the long-term rate would tend to rise relative to the shorter-term rate thus producing an upward-sloping yield curve. Under circumstances in which interest rates were expected to fall precisely the opposite kinds of shifts would tend to occur. Supply would shift from the short to the long-term market and demand from the long to the short-term market thus producing a rise in the short-term rate relative to the long-term rate and a downward sloping yield curve.

When allowance is made for the fact that the expectations of investors are uncertain and that they differ from one investor to another the precision of this expectational theory is destroyed. Nevertheless, it seems to explain broadly the pattern of movement of the interest rate structure. The diagram below illustrates these points.

Curve 1 is a yield curve where interest rates are expected to rise.

Curve 3 is a yield curve perhaps typical of a period where interest rates are high and are expected to fall.

Curve 2 is a yield curve in a period when interest rates are not expected to change.

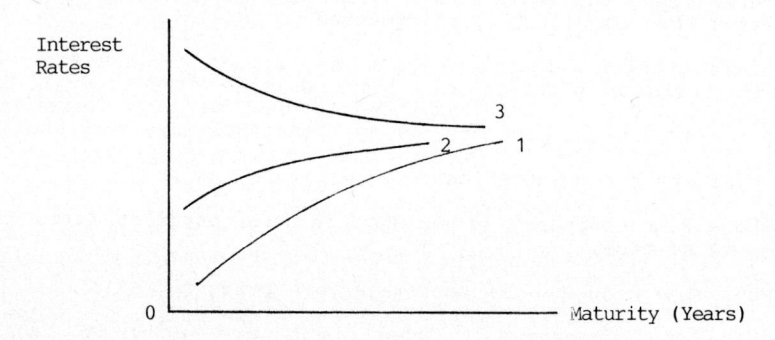

It is a fact that many lenders have a preference for liquidity and this will tend to depress the short-term rate below the long-term rate even when interest rates are not expected to change (Curve 2). Also there are limitations in the real world on the mobility of funds from one maturity sector to another and some lenders and borrowers have a preference for debt of certain maturities which interferes with the full realisation of the rate pattern that would be produced by the free reign of expectations.

In the UK, short rates have often been higher than long rates in the last few years reflecting the view that high short rates were expected to fall.

Time/yield curves of British government stocks

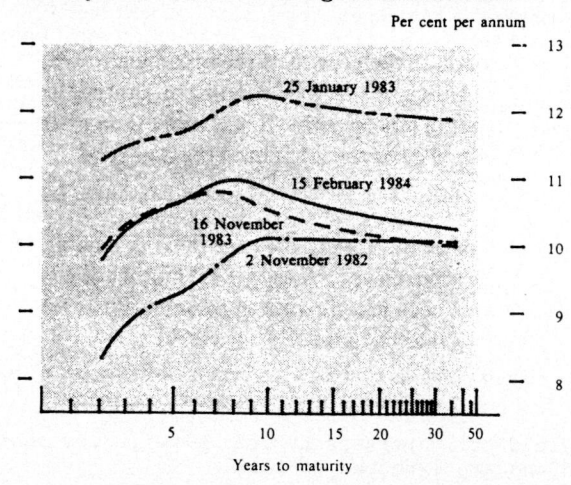

Source: Bank of England Quarterly Bulletin March 1984

CHAPTER 7   MONETARY TARGETING IN THE UK

Monetary targets in Britain:

Date Target Set	Period of Target	Aggregate	Target Growth Rate % p.a.	Actual Growth Rate % p.a.
December 1976	Year to April 77	£M3	9-13	17.7
March 1977	Year to April 78	"	9-13	16.0
April 1978	Year to April 79	"	8-12	10.9
November 1978	Year to Oct. 79	"	8-12	13.3
June 1979	June 79-April 80	"	7-11	10.3
November 1979	June 79-Oct. 80	"	7-11	17.8
March 1980	Feb 80-April 81	"	7-11	18.5
March 1981	Feb 81-April 82	"	6-10	14.5
March 1982	Feb 82-April 83	£M3 M1 PSL2	8-12	11.0 9.75 8.75
March 1983	Feb 83-April 84	£M3 M1 PSL2	7-11	9.7 11.1 12.8
March 1984	Feb 84-April 85	£M3 M0	6-10 4-8	

In addition, reducing target rates have been specified for the two aggregates £M3 and M0 for the remainder of the decade, as can be seen in the Table below.

Monetary Aggregate	1984/85	1985/86	1986/87	1987/88	1988/89
£M3 % p.a.	6-10	5-9	4-8	3-7	2-6
M0 % p.a.	4-8	3-7	2-6	1-5	0-4

Source: Bank of England Quarterly Bulletin March 1984

As already pointed out the authorities were paying more attention to the money stock in the 1970's but it wasn't until 1976 that it became the practice to announce targets regularly.

To give themselves more flexibility the authorities have set target ranges rather than point targets; the target rates have been gradually reduced over the years reflecting the desire of governments to reduce the rate of inflation. It is clear that the official targets have quite frequently not been achieved and the authorities have argued that on the occasions they weren't the performance of £M3 required interpretation in the light of other indicators including the exchange rate. There are a number of reasons why the monetary targets weren't always achieved.

1. Controlling measures of the money stock like £M3 is not an exact science; if it is done through interest rates the authorities have to estimate how much firms and households are likely to want to borrow from the banks and how this will change as interest rates change - it is clear that the Bank of England underestimated the strength of firms' demand for credit in the late 1970's and early 1980's. (Congdon 1982).

    A very important example here is the effect of prolonged inflationary uncertainty and high nominal interest rates on the pattern of corporate financing. "By the mid 1970's these pressures had for practical purposes forced corporate borrowers to abandon the market in long-term fixed interest debt. Although recourse to the equity market remained an option that continued to be used on a significant scale, medium term variable rate borrowing from banks became an attractive and readily available substitute for long-term bank financing. With the 'borrowing requirement' of the corporate sector being persistently large this tended substantially to increase the degree of banking intermediation and the growth of M3. Recently it has been counteracted by a debt-managment policy of "overfunding" by which the government borrows funds outside the banking sector that the corporate sector would formerly have borrowed directly and in effect uses them to finance variable-rate lending." (Bank of England September 1982).

2. The government doesn't always feel able to give priority to its monetary targets if these conflict with other objectives. One of the reasons that the 1977/78 target was exceeded was the authorities decision to cut interest rates in mid 1977 in an attempt to discourage capital outflows. It is clear that whilst the main target of monetary policy has been the growth of the money stock there have been occasions when, in setting interest rates, the authorities have given priority to the exchange rate.

3. The growth of the money stock may be inflated by special factors; Sterling M3 for example, was artificially boosted in 1981/82 by industrial action in the Civil Service which disrupted the collection of taxes.

4. The increase in personal savings and their flow to the business sector through the banks inflated M3 but without adverse effects for the future - this factor seems to have diminished in force recently.

5. In the early 1980's the performance of £M3 was affected first by a structural change following entry of the banks into the market for residential mortgages and second (but in the opposite direction) by the growth of foreign currency balances held by UK residents in preference to sterling. These structural changes were a lagged consequence of the abolition of exchange control in 1979 and of direct credit controls in 1980. The abolition of the 'corset' in 1980 served to give a boost to £M3 without significantly affecting expenditure. One effect of the 'corset' had been disintermediation, a particular form of which was the 'bill-leak'. Companies unable to raise funds that they needed issued commercial bills which when accepted were sold to the non-bank public; the companies received the funds that they needed and the net effect on the economy was much the same as if bank lending and the money stock had increased by the same amount. When the 'corset' was abolished firms ceased this particular form of financing and went back to bank loans with the effect of expanding £M3.

Any target chosen for monetary control should:

(a) be easy to identify and measure;

(b) give a reliable indication of monetary conditions;

(c) hold a predictable relationship with the final objective of policy;

(d) be relatively simple to control.

For much of the government's period of office the chosen target £M3 seemed to fulfill few of these conditions. For technical reasons, such as those above it didn't appear to give a true reflection of monetary conditions and the chosen technique of influencing the growth of £M3 - the manipulations of interest rates - was an imprecise mechanism. For example, demand for funds remained high in 1980 despite high interest rates. Changes in interest rates also impinge on other aspects of policy particularly the exchange rate. These difficulties persuaded the government to introduce multiple targets in the budget of 1982 covering M1, £M3 and PSL2 and to investigate the possibilities of developing another measure of the money supply which would be more appropriate as a means of predicting the subsequent growth in prices, M2. M2 is a classification of the money supply that seeks to concentrate on those deposits likely to be used as transactions balances and was first introduced by the Bank of England in 1982. M2 comprises notes and coins plus current account deposits and other deposits held by the private sector of less than £100,000 which can be withdrawn within one month. By identifying certain types of deposit according to size and maturity it is hoped that the new measure will be more directly related to transactions in goods and services than £M3 and somewhat less sensitive to relative interest rates than M1. This all represents a continual search on the part of the authorities for a target that will perform well and it is not surprising that the difficulties with £M3 should have provoked close interest in alternative target aggregates. If, for instance, another aggregate could have been found which had greatly superior behavioural characteristics then it might have been worth sacrificing the advantages derived from the accounting linkage of £M3 with government borrowing and bank lending.

M1 as a single target was not favoured because there is essentially only one instrument to control it with - the short-term rate of interest. "Neither the amount of interest rate change needed to secure a given change in the growth of M1 nor the length of time before the change can be secured can be estimated within reasonable limits. The rate of interest in this context is thus neither convincing nor reliable as an instrument and could as a result have had unacceptable side-effects on, for instance, the exchange rate." (Fforde, J.S.).

Radical change in the choice of target was considered for a number of years by the monetary authorities prior to 1981. The change debated was 'monetary base' control. Under this approach the central bank regulates closely the commercial banks' deposits (or balances) with itself. Commercial banks need to hold balances at the central bank since it is by transferring these balances that the banks make payments between themselves and also to the government, also it is by drawing on these balances that the banks can obtain more cash to meet withdrawals of cash by their customers. Because the banks need to hold balances with the central bank it may be possible to control the growth of the banks' lending and deposits by limiting the amount of these balances that are available to the banks. Another name for the banks' balances with the central bank is the 'monetary base' or 'base money' and this approach to the control of the money stock is often known as 'monetary base control'.

In fact it is more of a general term with a whole range of sub-species than a single specific technical construction. At one end it is the medium term targeting of the wide monetary base as described above; at the other end of the range it could amount to close control, perhaps almost week-to-week, over a monetary reserve base of the banks.

The arguments in favour of monetary base control did not prevail in 1980-81. It was, however, adopted as the narrow measure of the money supply in the Budget of 1984 together with £M3 as the wider measure.

The Bank of England argues:

1. That it wouldn't have been possible to carry out so determined a counter-inflationary strategy without monetary targets. "Use of strong intermediate targets for money supply and government borrowing enabled the authorities to stand back from output and employment as such and to stress the vital part to be played in respect of these by the trend of industrial costs .... they were vitally important at the outset in order to signal a decisive break with the past....". (Fforde 1983 op cit).

2. That the difficulties inherent in short-term monetary targetry are by no means fatal to the associated counter-inflationary strategy.... "For what matters is the refusal of the authorities to stimulate demand in 'Keynesian' fashion .... The fact the monetary targets have not been met is of much less importance. At one time it was feared that the difficulties encountered with M3 would leave the strategy bereft of a vital ingredient. Experience now suggests that this fear was exaggerated." (Fforde op cit).

But many commentators wonder:

1. Is it sufficient to continue with modified monetary targets, guidelines or 'expected ranges' for a year ahead accompanied by fiscal restraint or has it become desirable to indicate an acceptable medium-term path for nominal GDP too? A year ago the Bank of England argued it was time to do so. We now know that the Chancellor has decided against including it in his list of intermediate targets.

2. "Has modifying and qualifying the monetary target left us so prone to a weakening of counter-inflationary resolve that there is need for a very different intermediate target - namely the exchange rate as a sort of 'back-stop'". (Fforde op cit). This is the question that has been posed often in the last two years and again the Chancellor has announced his intention not to adopt it. It is argued that in the present international circumstances a 'fixed' exchange rate for sterling would make us extremely vulnerable to volatile short-term flows that would create unintended and intolerable side effects.

The experience of the last four years has been an exercise in British pragmatism. "It doesn't lack resolve, or a clear sense of direction but it recognises that the successful execution of monetary policy requires the exercise of judgement and a constantly interpretative approach to the evolving pattern of evidence.... This has been disappointing for those who distrust discretion and admire rules. But it is also disappointing for those who admire discretion and have no case for rules at all. The right balance has to be found empirically as we go along". (Fforde op cit).

APPENDIX 1   PROVISIONS OF COMPETITION AND CREDIT CONTROL

The reserve asset requirement

1. All banks with eligible liabilities of £5 million or more were required to maintain at least $12\frac{1}{2}$% of these liabilities in specified reserve assets. This requirement had to be observed on a daily basis.

2. In broad terms eligible liabilities were defined as:
   (i) sterling deposits of an original maturity of two years or less from the public; plus,
   (ii) sterling deposits from banks in the UK less any sterling claims on such banks; plus,
   (iii) sterling certificates of deposit issued less any holdings of such certificates; plus,
   (iv) any sterling resources obtained by switching foreign currencies into sterling.

3. Eligible reserve assets comprised:
   (i) balances with the Bank of England (other than special deposits);
   (ii) money at call with listed discount market institutions and listed brokers;
   (iii) treasury bills;
   (iv) local authority bills eligible for re-discount at the Bank of England;
   (v) commercial bills eligible for re-discount at the Bank of England (up to a maximum of 2% of eligible liabilities);
   (vi) government stocks and the stocks of nationalised industries guaranteed by the government with one year or less to final maturity.

4. Deposit-taking finance houses were also subject to the reserve asset requirement but for those institutions the minimum ratio was set at 10%.

Special deposits

5. Banks and deposit-taking finance houses were periodically obliged to place balances at the Bank of England equal to a specified proportion of their eligible liabilities. These special deposits earned interest at a rate equivalent to treasury bill rate.

Ratio controls on the Discount Houses

6.   The discount houses were obliged to hold at least 50% of their borrowed funds in the following specified public sector assets: treasury bills; local authority bills and bonds; government and local authority stocks with not more than 5 years to final maturity. Because of distortions that this regulation generated (in particular when the discount houses were close to the limit set by the ratio, the rates on the public sector assets in question were sometimes bid extremely low) the requirement was changed in 1973. Since discount houses have had to limit their holdings of 'non-specified' - essentially private sector - assets to a maximum of 20 times their capital and reserves.*

* In early 1981 this limit was raised to a maximum of 25 times their capital and reserves.

Source: Banking Information Service, Institute of Bankers.

APPENDIX 2   THE EXPECTATIONS-AUGMENTED PHILLIPS CURVE
AND THE NATURAL RATE OF UNEMPLOYMENT

The basic doctrine inherent in the Expectations-Augmented Phillips curve is that there is an underlying rate of unemployment (and of output growth) in the economy which is the best that can be achieved for a time; it is achieved when the rate of inflation is stable. The level of unemployment may be unsatisfactory but it can only be changed by structural reforms of markets which are working badly; it cannot be reduced by the usual aggregate demand reflationary methods which, it is argued, will only lead to accelerating inflation.

This minimum sustainable rate of unemployment was labelled the 'natural' rate by Phelps (1967) and Friedman (1969). Another name for it occasionally used is the 'constant inflation rate of unemployment' (C.I.R.); yet another label used by Professor R.Layard of the LSE is the 'critical' level of unemployment.

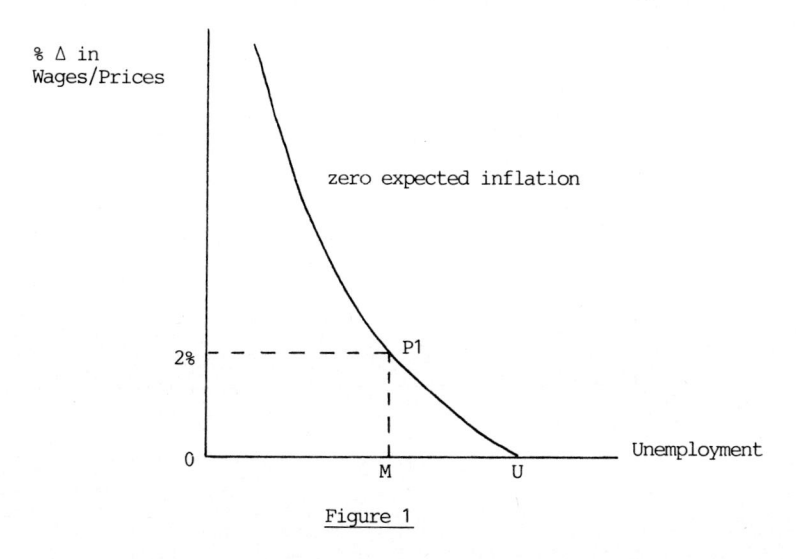

Figure 1

Figure 1 is a conventional Phillips curve drawn on the assumption of zero-expected inflation. It suggests that if unemployment is at OU there will be no change in wages and inflation will be zero.

- 41 -

What happens if OU unemployment is deemed too high by the government and aggregate demand is boosted to reduce it? If money illusion exists unemployment will drop, say to OM and the price level will rise by, say, 2%. The assumption was that the economy would settle there, at point P1, i.e. that there was a trade-off that could be achieved between unemployment and price stability.

As we all know the Phillips curve became extremely misleading by the end of the 1960's - early 1970's - rising unemployment and rising inflation could not be explained by it. In the circumstances a new explanation was developed that laid stress on people's expectations about the future.

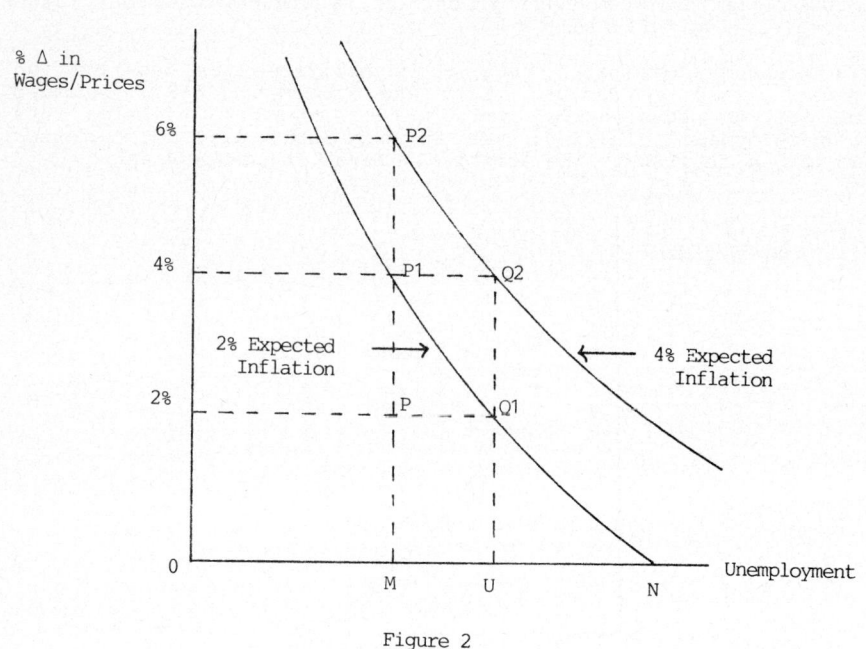

Figure 2

In Figure 2 workers no longer suffer from money illusion and after the 2% rise in the price level associated with the fall in unemployment they insist on higher wages to counter the rise in the cost of living - in other words the economy moves to P1; this is an expectations-augmented Phillips curve incorporating the belief that prices will rise by 2%. In the next round the workers

- 42 -

ask for 4% - the inflation rate adjusts to 4% and the economy moves to P2. Once this happens workers ask for 6% and as long as unemployment is kept at OM by the government continuing to boost demand, inflation will continue to accelerate. The trade-off in other words is no longer between unemployment and a measure of inflation as in Figure 1 but between unemployment and accelerating inflation.

Should the government be prepared to settle for whatever rate of inflation has emerged when it abandons its demand boosting experiment it will have to allow unemployment to return to at least OU. Thus in the long-run the Phillips curve is a vertical line going through U, Q1, Q2 and there is no long-term trade-off between unemployment and inflation. By allowing unemployment to rise again the government destroys the inflationary expectations that have been generated, the inflation rate will thus stabilise and cease to accelerate. It follows that if the government should want to reduce the inflation rate it will have to allow the level of unemployment to rise beyone OU, perhaps significantly so. The level of unemployment at which the inflation rate stabilises, i.e. below which inflation accelerates, is what is known as the natural rate of unemployment and it is through this point that the vertical long-run Phillips curve runs. In Figure 2 above, the causal links went from a boost to demand to a fall in unemployment, to a rise in wages to a rise in prices.

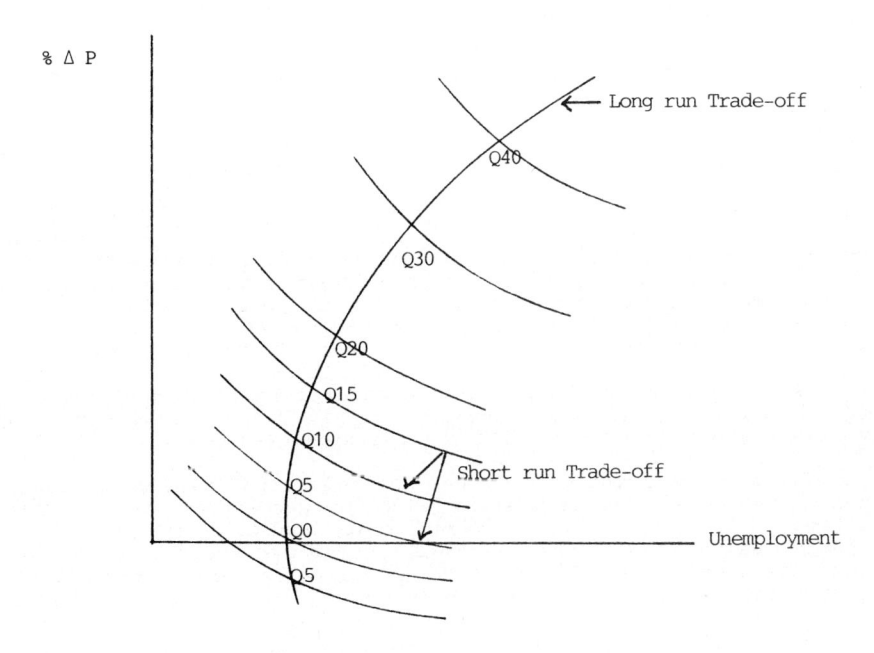

% Δ P

Long run Trade-off

Q40

Q30

Q20

Q15

Q10

Q5

Q0

Q5

Short run Trade-off

Unemployment

Figure 3

Source: S.Brittan "How to End the Monetarist Controversy" Hobart Paper 190 IEA 1981 Page 58

- 43 -

What can be said then of the relationship between unemployment and inflation? The message of the expectations-augmented Phillips curve is that there is a short-run trade-off - a fall in unemployment will be accompanied by a rise in inflation, a reduction in inflation may require very high levels of unemployment. In the long-run there is either no relation at all or - at very high rates of inflation - an opposite relation where high rates of inflation are associated with high rates of unemployment. (Brittan 1981).

In Figure 3 above, point 0Q0 is close to the natural rate of unemployment. The short-run Phillips curves show that the initial stages of an anti-inflationary programme will lead to a temporary rise in unemployment and that any attempt to reduce unemployment will be matched by a rise in the price level. It must be stressed that there are no simple proportional relationships involved however: we cannot predict by how much unemployment must rise to bring about a specified reduction in inflation and the steps by which the economy moves from the short-term to the long-term Phillips curve will vary widely according to the particular circumstances of each cycle.

As Brittan points out, steady rates of inflation of 20, 30 or 50% are unknown thus the higher reaches of the long-run Phillips curve are best regarded as representing averages around which the rate of inflation oscillates and a large part of the long-run unemployment costs arise from the instability and unpredictability of actual rates of inflation when the average rate is high.

Brittan also points out that typically graphs such as that above represent changes coming only from the demand (or MV) side. However, there are many forces on the supply (or PT) side which can boost prices in the short-term and also raise unemployment - for example, the oil-price explosions of 1973-74 and 1979-80. In other words graphical representations such as those above don't preclude rises in the price level without favourable effects on unemployment. And, of course, events may occur which serve to shift the long-term Phillips curve to the right and worsen unemployment with no reduction in inflation even in the short-run.

This is a good point to look at the natural level of unemployment, to see why it is at a particular level at a particular time, and to see how or why it may shift its position over time.

It will be remembered that it was defined as the rate of unemployment which would be consistent with an unchanging rate of inflation: a level of unemployment that couldn't be permanently reduced using conventional aggregate demand reflationary policies. The actual position of the curve at any time is associated with institutional rigidities in the economy and can only be shifted by, for example, the structural reform of markets that are working badly. The policy implication of this is that the natural rate can only be reduced by using micro-economic policies rather than macro-economic policies, that is by working on the supply side of the economy. This is sometimes called the Market Approach. Some of the more important rigidities determining the natural rate are associated with the housing market, the tax and social security system and with labour monopoly power. For example: "The social security and tax system has two potential effects on work incentives. It establishes a floor wage below which it is not worth taking a registered job. But, even for people with a wage above the floor, the net gain from taking a job is reduced by the combination of lower benefit and liability to tax which constitutes the poverty trap". (Brittan, S. 1981). Other commentators, whilst making the same points, go even further and argue that if unemployment is to be reduced in the forseeable future then the programme to improve the operation of the market will have to be speeded up. They call for "increasing incentives by cuts in marginal tax rates, the return of activities to the private sector (Privatisation), increasing the scope of competition both in the public and private sector and sharp reduction in union monopoly power". (Minford, P. 1981).

The economic policies of the Conservative government of 1979, re-elected in 1983, indicate an acceptance of the natural rate hypothesis. Other political parties have advocated gradual expansionary policies at least, but without a coherent economic rationale to counter the natural rate. However, a paper by R.Cross (1983) outlines a formulation of the natural rate theory which provides "good reason" to expect that expansionary demand policies would achieve a sustained reduction in unemployment without being accompanied by ever-increasing inflation. His formulation rests on the adoption of the hysteresis version of the natural rate theory outline by Phelps (1972) whereby the natural rate depends on the history of aggregate demand. "The transition from one equilibrium to the other tends to have long-lingering effects on the labour force and these effects may be discernable in the equilibrium unemployment rate for a long time. The natural unemployment rate at any future date will depend upon the course of history in the interim. Such a property is sometimes called hysteresis". (Phelps 1972).

Phelps outlined two hysteresis effects. The first relates to the way the employment experience of the labour force helps shape the characteristics of the labour force. The argument here rests on the theory that longer or more frequent spells of unemployment tend to make people less employable rather than allow those unemployed to acquire new skills and habits which are conducive to employment. To the extent that government re-training and work experience schemes are successful the effects of this hysteresis process in raising the natural rate of unemployment will be reduced.

The second effect relates to the role of trade unions. "A rise in employment is postulated to be accompanied by a rise in the numbers employed in jobs covered by trade unions. This increase in union employment is postulated to reduce the mark-ups that trade unions can achieve over non-union jobs: higher union employment is achieved at the cost of lower union mark-ups. Thus higher employment will reduce any component of the natural rate of unemployment associated with the relative price distortions arising from union mark-ups". (Cross, R. 1983). It should be said that the existence of this hysteresis effect is open to serious question (Oswald, A. 1979; Bain, E and Elsheik, F. 1976). The hysteresis effect concentrated upon in the paper by Cross (1983) operates through changes in aggregate demand changing the number of long-term unemployed in the labour force. He argues that long-term unemployment debilitates the people concerned and atrophies the capacity to work and that as a result changes in long-term unemployment lead to parallel changes in the natural rate of unemployment. He argues that this hysteresis theory provides a coherent account of why expansionary aggregate demand policies can achieve a sustained reduction in unemployment without leading to ever-increasing inflation.

NOTES

1. In the development of the theory Keynes used the rate of return on a fixed interest government bond (a financial asset) to act as 'r'. Given that rates of interest tend to move together in the same direction, even if at different speeds, it is convenient to have one asset to act as a proxy for all assets.

2. Perhaps the best basic text dealing with these topics is The Demand for Money - Theories and Evidence by David E.W. Laidler 2nd Ed. Dun-Donnelley Publishing Corporation 1977.

3. Professor Alan Budd (1980) goes for a very broad definition of monetarism. "I can include in my survey many who would normally be most surprised to find themselves described as "monetarists". I shall include all those who are prepared to credit money with some economic role and I shall divide them into three groups. The first I shall describe as "Primitive Monetarists". This group is particularly associated with Friedman. The second group consists of the New Classical School. That School tends to be identified with belief in rational expectations. However it is possible to believe in the R.E.H. without subscribing to all the views of the New Classical School. The third group I shall call the Eclectic Monetarists. It includes the group normally known as Neo-Keynesians including Tobin, Solow and Buiter. By British standards these economists are monetarists. I should emphasise that all these labels are entirely arbitrary. To illustrate this a recent report by Minford (1980) classified the London Business School, The National Institute and the Treasury jointly as Neo-Keynesians".
See also Douglas D. Purvis (1980).

4. The fundamental idea of rational expectations is that if a model incorporates expectations it must do so in a way that is consistent with the model itself. In other words the model builder cannot assume that he understands how the economy works but that no one else does. The idea of Rational Expectations is by no means new and its application to macroeconomics now dates back over a decade. Originally the approach was used to launch a major attack on conventional econometric models.

In the classic paper by Sargant and Wallace (1975) they arrive at the view that monetary policy can work by surprising people; but such an exercise would be pointless. They conclude that the best monetary policy is one that follows a well-defined simple growth rule.

Sargant and Wallace seem therefore to have reached the same conclusion as Friedman, namely that monetary policy should not be used for stabilisation. However they give a very different reason. Where Friedman argues that stabilisation policy should not be attempted because no one can forecast the behaviour of the economy, Sargant and Wallace argue that it should not be attempted because everyone can forecast the economy.

I should add here that it isn't necessary to subscribe to REH to be a 'monetarist'. Laidler (1982) argues strongly against the hypothesis whilst still insisting on the importance of price expectations as such and more generally on the fact that some people in markets anticipate and react quickly to changes in government policies. In particular he argues that the distinction between anticipated and unanticipated monetary growth is important and the ways in which monetary changes affect the economy will be influenced by the ways in which different markets react. More particularly he concludes that the transmissions mechanism may well vary as behaviour varies in the light of what people conceive policy to be.
Also on Rational Expectations read: R.Maddock and M.Carter (1982) and P.Minford and D.Peel (1981).

5. The definitive articles on the institutional arrangements for the implementation of monetary policy are to be found in the Bank of England Quarterly Bulletin (March 1982, Coleby June 1982 and Fforde June 1983).

6. For a very readable explanation of this process see Livesey,F 1982.

7. For those wanting to read more on the money markets I would recommend books by E.R.Shaw (1981) and A.D.Bain (1981).

8. The Certificate of Deposit is a certificate stating that a deposit of a certain amount has been placed with a bank for a given period and at a fixed or floating rate of interest. It is a negotiable asset so that a depositor who holds it can resell it in a secondary market.

REFERENCES

Bain A D	The Economics of the Financial System	Martin-Robertson 1981
Bank of England	'The role of the Bank of England in the money market'	B o E Q.B. March 1982
Bank of England	'Yield Curves for gilt-edged stocks: an improved model'	B o E Q.B. June 1982
Bank of England	'Setting Monetary Objectives'	B o E Q.B. Sept 1982
Brittan S	How to Solve the Monetarist Controversy	Institute of Economic Affairs 1981
Brunner K	'The Case against Monetary Activism'	Lloyds Bank Review January 1981
Budd A	'Recent Developments in Monetarism'	British Review of Economic Issues Nov. 1980 Vol 2 No.7
Coleby A L	'The Bank's operational procedures for meeting monetary objectives'	B o E Q.B. June 1982
Congdon T	'Why has monetarism failed so far? The missed targets'	The Banker March 1982
Cross R	Long-Term Unemployment, Hysteresis and the Natural Rate of Unemployment	The Business Economist Summer 1983
Davies A	'Living without MLR. The move to "flexible" interest rates'	Barclays Review No.1 February 1982
Davies A	'Monetary Economics'	Banking World Feb.1984
Dennis C E J	'Rationale of Monetary Policy' in The Framework of UK Monetary Economics by D T Llewellyn, C E J Dennis, M J B Hall and J E Nellis	Heinemann Educational Books 1982
Fforde J S	'Setting Monetary Objectives'	B o E Q.B. June 1983
Friedman M	'The Role of Monetary Policy'	The American Economic Review March 1968
Goodhart C A E	'The Importance of Money' in Readings in British Monetary Economics by H E Johnson (ed)	Clarendon Press 1972
Johnson H G	Macroeconomics and Monetary Theory	Basil Blackwood Oxford 1978
Laidler D E W	The Demand for Money: Theories and Evidence	Dunn-Donnelley Publishing Corporation 2nd Edition 1977
Laidler D E W	'Monetarism: An Interpretation and an Assessment'	Economic Journal (91) March 1981

Laidler D E W	Monetarist Perspectives	Phillip Allan 1982
Lipsey R E	An Introduction to Positive Economics	Weidenfeld and Nicholson 1983
Livesey F	A Textbook of Economics	Polytechnic Publishers 1982 2nd Ed.
Maddock R & Carter M	'A Child's Guide to Rational Expectations'	Journal of Economic Literature March 1982
Minford P & Peel D	'Is the Government's Economic Strategy on Course?'	Lloyds Bank Review April 1981
Phelps E S	'Phillips Curves, Expectations of Inflation and Optimal Unemploymnet over time'	Economica August 1963
Phelps E S	Inflation Policy and Unemployment Theory	MacMillan 1972
Purvis D D	'Monetarism: A Review'	Canadian Journal of Economics XII No.1 February 1980
Sargant T & Wallace N	'Rational Expectations, the Optimal Monetary Instrument and the Optimal Money Supply Rule'	Journal of Political Economy 83 (2) 1975
Shaw E R	The London Money Market	Heinemann London 1981
Smith W I	'The Maturity Structure of Interest Rates' in Readings in Money, National Income and Stabilisation Policy 3rd Ed. by W I Smith & R L Teigen	Richard D Irwin Inc. 1974